SOLVING MYSTERIES WITH SCIENCE

THE BERMUDA TRIANGLE

JANE BINGHAM

Chicago, Illinois

© 2013 Heinemann Raintree
an imprint of Capstone Global Library, LLC
Chicago, Illinois

To contact Capstone Global Library please
phone 800-747-4992, or visit our website
www.capstonepub.com

Edited by Adam Miller and Abby Colich
Designed by Marcus Bell
Original illustrations (pages 7, 11,15) © Chris King
2013
All other original illustrations © Capstone Global
Library
Illustrated by Chris King and HL Studios
Picture research by Mica Brancic
Originated by Capstone Global Library, Ltd.

Printed in the United States of America
3392

**Library of Congress Cataloging-in-Publication
Data**
Bingham, Jane.

Bermuda Triangle / Jane Bingham.
p. cm.—(Solving mysteries with science)
Includes bibliographical references and index.
ISBN 978-1-4109-4986-8 (hb)—ISBN
978-1-4109-4991-2 (pb)
1. Bermuda Triangle—Juvenile literature. 2. Shipwrecks—Bermuda Triangle—Juvenile literature. I.
Title.
G558.B56 2013
001.94—dc23   2012012694

Acknowledgments

The author and publisher are grateful to the following
for permission to reproduce copyright material:Alamy:
pp. 21 (© Stocktrek Images, Inc), 22 (© Saverio Maria
Gallotti), 26 (© Michael Patrick O'Neill), 31 (© US
Coast Guard Photo), 39 (© Prisma Bildagentur AG),
42 (© Mary Evans Picture Library); Corbis: pp. 23
(All Canada Photos/© Robert Postma), 24 (© Tim
Davis), 25 top (© John Lund), 27 (© Image Source),
30 top (© Julian Calverley), 37 (© Bettmann); Getty
Images: 32 (Photographer's Choice/Aaron Foster),
38 (The Agency Collection/Dorling Kindersley);
iStockphoto: p. 34 (© Linda Bucklin); Newscom: p. 35
main photo (DanitaDelimont.com "Danita Delimont
Photography"/Greg Johnston); Rex Features: p. 33
(Everett Collection); Science Photo Library: p. 18
(NASA); Shutterstock: pp. 4 (© Mikael Damkier), 19
(© Kisialiou Yury), 20 (© J.Schelkle), 25 bottom (©
Kaarsten), 28 (© Eric Gevaert), 29 top (© Tischenko
Irina), 29 bottom (© Tatiana Popova), 30 bottom (©
Nino Cavalier), 36 top (© Doglikehorse), 36 top (©
Kompaniets Taras), 36 bottom (© forbis), 40 (© Bruce
C. Murray), 41 main photo (© Ramunas Bruzas), 43
(© Ilja Mašík).

Cover photographs: airplane above the clouds
reproduced with permission from Shutterstock (©
Mikael Damkier); blue sea with waves and clear blue
sky reproduced with permission from Shutterstock
(© Dudarev Mikhail); Bermuda Triangle conceptual
computer artwork reproduced with permission from
Getty Images (Science Photo Library/Victor Habbick
Visions).

Design feature images: Shutterstock.

CONTENTS

What Is the Bermuda Triangle? 4
The Fate of Flight 19 6
Disappearing Crews 10
Terror in the Clouds 14
Investigating the Triangle 18
Weird Weather? 20
An Unusual Ocean? 24
Scientific Explanations? 28
Aliens and Atlantis? 32
Human Causes? 36
Is There Really a Mystery? 40
Can the Mystery Be Solved? 42
Timeline 44
Summing Up the Science 45
Glossary 46
Find Out More 47
Index 48

WHAT IS THE BERMUDA TRIANGLE?

For centuries, travelers have feared the stretch of Atlantic Ocean known as the Bermuda Triangle. Dozens of ships and planes have disappeared inside this mysterious region never to be seen again. Inside the Bermuda Triangle, storms blow up from nowhere, pilots and sailors become lost and confused, and the laws of nature seem to be suspended. No one is safe in these waters. Or so it seems...

Where is the Bermuda Triangle?

The area of ocean known as the Bermuda Triangle covers roughly 500,000 square miles (1.3 million square kilometers). It lies between three points: Miami Beach, in Florida, the town of San Juan, Puerto Rico, and the island of Bermuda. Many small islands lie inside the Triangle, but for most of its expanse it is simply uninterrupted water.

Many theories

Dozens of theories have been put forward to explain the mystery of the Bermuda Triangle. Some people blame freak storms, giant waves, or strange fogs and gases. Others think unusual force fields are at work, making compasses swing wildly out of control. Some people claim that the buried city of Atlantis has a mysterious power over the waters above it. Some writers have even suggested that ships and planes are snatched up by aliens and beamed to another planet!

Can the mystery be solved?

In the first part of this book, you can learn about the fate of people who have perished inside the Triangle. You can also read the chilling account of a pilot who managed to survive a near-death experience.

The second part of this book takes a careful look at the theories behind the disappearances and asks some questions. Do the theories make sense? Have the so-called experts approached the problem in a scientific way? And can science solve the mystery of the Bermuda Triangle?

MANY NAMES

The Bermuda Triangle has been called the Sea of Doom, the Graveyard of the Atlantic, and the Devil's Triangle.

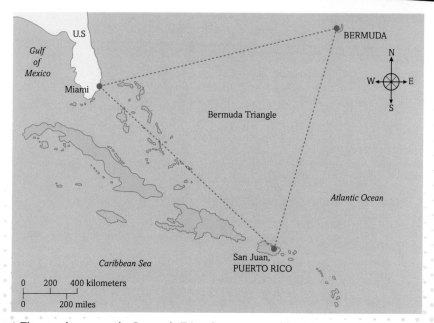

▲ The area known as the Bermuda Triangle covers roughly 500,000 square miles (1.3 million square kilometers). It lies between the island of Bermuda, San Juan in Puerto Rico, and Miami in Florida.

THE FATE OF FLIGHT 19

On the afternoon of December 5, 1945, 13 young men gathered at Fort Lauderdale, Florida. They were the crew of Flight 19, a squadron of five U.S. navy planes. They were preparing for a routine training exercise led by their instructor, Lieutenant Charles Taylor.

A SIMPLE EXERCISE

As the pilots waited on the runway, they ran through the steps of their exercise. First, they would fly east for 56 miles (90 kilometers). Then, they would release their training bombs into the sea. They would then continue east for another 67 miles (108 kilometers), before changing course and heading north for 73 miles (117 kilometers). Finally, they would turn southwest and fly the 120 miles (193 kilometers) back to their base in Fort Lauderdale.

The whole operation would last just two hours. The weather was fine, and all five planes had been thoroughly checked.

What could possibly go wrong?

"I DON'T KNOW WHERE WE ARE..."

At first, everything went according to plan. The crews took off at 2:10 p.m., completed their bombing practice, and continued flying east. But then a disturbing silence filled the airwaves.

Up until this time, the planes had been in regular contact with base. But nothing was heard from Flight 19 for 40 long minutes. Meanwhile, the weather was changing and heavy black clouds were gathering overhead.

At last, another pilot who was flying nearby picked up a signal. Lieutenant Robert Cox tuned his radio and heard Lieutenant Taylor talking to one of his pilots. Cox felt his blood run cold as he heard the chilling words, "I don't know where we are. We must have got lost after that last turn." Something had gone horribly wrong.

"IT LOOKS LIKE WE ARE ENTERING WHITE WATER!"

Cox tried desperately to contact Taylor, but it was 20 minutes before he heard his voice on the radio again. This time, Taylor sounded panicked and confused. His compass had failed, and he thought he might be flying over an area called the Florida Keys. Cox responded fast, telling Taylor to head north toward the Florida coast.

It was good advice, but it did not work. In less than five minutes, Taylor radioed back saying he couldn't see land. Then some other voices came over the radio. This time, there was no mistaking their sense of fear. One of the men said desperately, "We're completely lost!" Another shouted out in alarm, "It looks like we are entering white water!"

Flight 19 seemed to be heading straight for disaster. What exactly was this patch of white water? And where could it be? There was nothing anyone could do to help.

INTO THE VOID

By 5:00 p.m., it was horribly clear that Taylor was losing his grip on reality. He was no longer listening to radio instructions. Instead, he issued a series of confusing commands. First, he ordered his students to fly due east. Forty minutes later, he turned the squadron (group of planes) around and headed west. But after just a few minutes, he turned east again. Radio signals slowly died away, and Flight 19 was never seen again...

DISASTER STRIKES AGAIN

Shortly after 5 p.m., two seaplanes set off to search for Flight 19. Less than half an hour later, the crew of a nearby oil tanker heard a deafening explosion. Gazing up at the sky, they watched in horror as a burning seaplane plummeted into the sea. All 13 airmen died instantly. The deadly Bermuda Triangle had claimed another set of victims.

DISAPPEARING CREWS

Many strange things have happened inside the Bermuda Triangle. But one of the weirdest of all took place over a century ago. Back in the winter of 1881, the crew of a ship called the *Ellen Austin* saw a sight they would never forget...

A MYSTERIOUS MIST

It was over a month since the *Ellen Austin* had left England, heading for the United States. The crew had suffered a rough winter crossing, and they heaved a sigh of relief as they sailed past the Bahamas. They were all looking forward to an easy voyage home.

But almost as soon as they entered the Bermuda Triangle, a mysterious mist descended over the ocean. Cautiously, the crew sailed onward, when suddenly the lookout boy gave a startled cry of "Ship ahoy!"

Peering through the mist, the sailors could just make out a tall and graceful schooner sailing toward them.

A GHOSTLY SHIP

The sailors let out a cheer and waited for an answering shout. But nothing came. All that could be heard was the creaking of timbers as the schooner sailed on silently through the waves.

Gradually, the mist cleared, and the ship came into view. The sailors rubbed their eyes. Could it really be true? There was no crew on board, but the schooner was sailing smoothly. Slowly, the horrible truth dawned on them. They were staring at a ghost ship!

"BOARD THAT SHIP!"

On board the *Ellen Austin*, the sailors gazed at the ghost ship in horror. What could have happened to the unlucky crew? It was a mystery. But they knew they needed to get away as fast as they could.

Unfortunately, their captain had other ideas. "Board that ship!" he ordered. "I want a crew of my finest men to sail it to New York."

THE SHIP IS LOST

Soon the ghost ship had a new crew and was sailing beside the *Ellen Austin*. But it was not out of danger. Without any warning, a violent storm blew up, and both ships were rocked by powerful winds. After two days, the storm finally died down. But when the crew of the *Ellen Austin* looked around for the ghost ship, it was nowhere to be seen.

For the next few days, the *Ellen Austin* sailed the waters of the Bermuda Triangle, searching for the missing schooner.

Each day, the crew scanned the ocean with sinking hearts, certain that the ship must have been wrecked.

VANISHED INTO THIN AIR

Eventually, the captain gave orders to head for home, when suddenly a shout came from the lookout boy. The crew strained their eyes and saw the sight they had been longing for. A familiar ship came sailing calmly toward them, totally undamaged by the storm.

The sailors burst into cheers of joy. But soon their cries of delight changed to gasps of horror. As the ship came nearer, they saw that once again it was deserted—all their fellow crew members were gone. Scrambling on board, the sailors found the ghost ship in perfect order. There was no sign that the men had left in a panic.

They had simply vanished into thin air...

TERROR IN THE CLOUDS

It was a clear, sunny day in December 1970 when Bruce Gernon prepared his small plane for takeoff. He was taking two passengers on a sightseeing flight around the Bahamas. But what started off as a pleasure trip rapidly descended into a nightmare.

OMINOUS CLOUDS

As he left the runway, Gernon noticed a weird-looking cloud straight in front of him. He climbed steeply to avoid it, but it was keeping up with him, rising higher and higher until it completely surrounded his plane.

For 10 anxious minutes, Gernon plowed through the cloud, until at last his plane emerged into clear skies.

He breathed a sigh of relief, but the flight's problems had only just begun.

A second cloud was forming directly ahead of the plane, rising out of the sea like an inky tower.

TRAPPED IN THE CLOUDS

As soon as Gernon entered the cloud, everything went black. Then blinding flashes of light lit up the sky. He had flown through plenty of storm clouds before, but this was different—and he knew he had to get out fast.

Swerving sharply, he broke into a clear patch of sky. But then he realized he had not escaped. The plane was trapped inside a tube of clouds, and the walls of the tube were closing in on it!

A GAP IN THE CLOUDS

For the next few desperate minutes, Gernon struggled not to panic, until he spotted something that gave him hope—a tiny gap in the wall of cloud.

Gernon headed quickly for the gap. But then, in front of his eyes, it started changing shape. Slowly, the gap changed into a perfect circle, forming the entrance to a tunnel. He aimed straight for the circle, but it was shrinking fast. Could he and his passengers make it out alive?

OUT OF THE TUNNEL

It felt like Gernon and his passengers would never reach the end of the tunnel, but at last they were out. Looking back, Gernon gasped out loud as he saw the circle turn into a slit and then disappear. Then he forced himself to concentrate on the dangers ahead.

AN "ELECTRONIC FOG"

The plane was surrounded by a grayish haze. All of Gernon's navigation instruments (electronic tools to help him find his way) had failed, and his compass was spinning gently, even though he was flying straight.

Desperately, he contacted the communication tower to find out his position,

but no one could locate him. The plane seemed to be lost inside an electronic fog.

TRAVELING THROUGH TIME?

Gernon continued flying blind for three long minutes, until a voice crackled over his radio, saying, "We've located your plane over Miami Beach, Florida."

Gernon checked his watch. It was incredible. He had been flying for less than 40 minutes, and yet he had covered a distance that usually took him an hour and a half. Had he managed to travel through some kind of time warp?

Meanwhile, his view was finally starting to clear. He rubbed his eyes in amazement as Miami Beach came into view. Minutes later, he was landing his plane. The flight would haunt him for the rest of his life.

INVESTIGATING THE TRIANGLE

Can the mystery of the Bermuda Triangle be solved? People have put forward a range of different theories to explain the strange events that take place inside the Triangle. But do these theories stand up to investigation? The next six chapters will consider the theories and put them to the test of science and common sense.

Is there really a mystery?

Some people claim that all the weird events can be explained by science or common sense. You can read their arguments on pages 40 and 41.

The Triangle is born

There have been reports of weird events in the Bermuda region for centuries. But it was not until the 1950s that the idea of a deadly "Bermuda Triangle" was born. In 1952, a U.S. journalist named George X. Sand wrote an article for *Fate*, a magazine that investigated unexplained events. Sand listed several ships and planes that had disappeared in "a watery triangle bounded roughly by Florida, Bermuda, and Puerto Rico." His article led to a surge of theories about the Bermuda Triangle. Interest in the Triangle reached its peak in the 1970s, but some investigators are still at work today.

THE SCIENTIFIC METHOD

Good investigators follow the scientific method when they need to establish and test a theory. The scientific method has five basic steps:

1. Make observations (comments based on studying something closely).
2. Do some background research.
3. Form a testable hypothesis. This is basically a prediction or "educated guess" to explain the observations.
4. Conduct experiments or find evidence to support the hypothesis.
5. After thinking carefully about the evidence, draw conclusions.

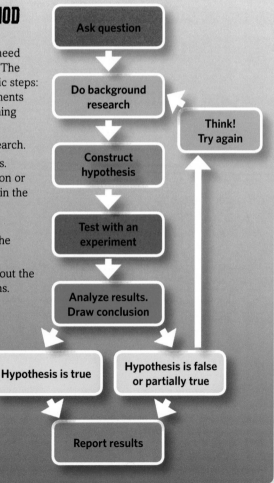

Ask question

Do background research

Think! Try again

Construct hypothesis

Test with an experiment

Analyze results. Draw conclusion

Hypothesis is true

Hypothesis is false or partially true

Report results

WEIRD WEATHER?

Accounts of strange events in the Triangle often include descriptions of very unusual weather. Survivors have described mysterious fogs, mists, and clouds, flashing lights in the sky, and terrifying winds or waves that seem to come from nowhere. Many reports of disasters stress that people started a journey on a perfectly calm day and then met weird weather with no warning at all. This chapter will investigate unusual weather in the Triangle area.

Myth-buster

Mysterious mists?

People who write about the Triangle often mention the spooky character of the mists and fogs that suddenly surround a ship or plane. But are they really so mysterious? Thick mists and fogs are very common in the Triangle region. They are caused when warm air meets cold water. The water in the air is forced to cool rapidly and forms small droplets, creating a mist or fog that hovers over the ocean.

▲ Thick sea mists are a common sight inside the Bermuda Triangle.

▲ This satellite image shows a powerful hurricane swirling over the ocean.

Storms at sea

The Bermuda Triangle region is battered by frequent tropical storms, also known as hurricanes or cyclones. Tropical storms can develop over the ocean with very little warning, and winds can quickly pick up speed to 40 miles (64 kilometers) per hour or more. A ship or plane caught inside a cyclone is suddenly surrounded by whirling wind and thunderclouds and hit by driving rain. Cyclones at sea also create gigantic waves, putting ships and boats in great danger.

Normal or paranormal?

Some investigators claim that the weird weather in the Triangle is a sign that paranormal forces are at work. But is this hypothesis correct? In fact, the Triangle area is well known for its extreme and changeable weather. It is not unusual for brilliant sunshine and clear blue skies to be replaced in minutes by terrifying thunderstorms and violent winds.

Waterspouts

Stormy weather over tropical seas can result in a waterspout. Waterspouts are formed when low thunderclouds make contact with the ocean, creating a vertical (up-and-down) column of spinning cloud. They travel over the ocean at speeds of up to 40 to 50 miles (64 to 80 kilometers) per hour, picking up any floating objects in their path.

Waterspouts can pose a serious threat to swimmers and small boats. They may have caused some unexplained disasters in the Triangle area.

▲ Waterspouts are very common in the Bermuda Triangle. In fact, the ocean around the Florida Keys is sometimes called "the waterspout capital of the world."

Myth-buster

Faulty forecasts

Writers often claim that the weather forecast was clear at the time of a disappearance in the Triangle. But weather forecasts cannot accurately predict what happens out at sea. Even today, with satellite cameras, it is easy to fail to spot storms at sea. There is a 12-hour gap between the time a weather satellite passes over a specific spot on the globe until the time it passes again. During these hours, a brief but violent storm can develop out at sea and then run out of power.

Rogue waves

Rogue waves strike out of the blue. They are at least double the size of all the waves around them. Some have been estimated to be as tall as 80 feet (24 meters)—the height of an eight-story building. Rogue waves can cause enormous damage, even sinking ocean liners. Oceanographers (people who study oceans) believe that some disappearances in the Triangle could have been the result of an encounter with a rogue wave.

HOW ARE ROGUE WAVES FORMED?

No single cause has been discovered for rogue waves, but it is thought that they are linked to powerful ocean currents. A current called the Gulf Stream (see page 25), which runs through the Bermuda Triangle, is a possible cause of rogue waves in the region.

AN UNUSUAL OCEAN?

Many Triangle investigators have pointed out the strange character of the ocean in this region. Some have described how vessels have been caught in powerful currents and sent completely off course. Some have noted blue holes on the ocean floor around the Bahamas and claimed that they could be portals (entrances) to another world. A few imaginative writers have told dramatic tales of attacks by sea monsters or killer seaweed. All these elements sound very mysterious, but can they in fact be explained by science?

Myth-buster

Sea monsters or sharks?

No evidence has been found of mysterious sea monsters in the waters of the Bermuda Triangle area, but this part of the North Atlantic Ocean is home to deadly sharks and vicious fish called barracudas. The tiger shark and the bull shark are both native to the area and are greatly feared because of their attacks on swimmers.

Caught in the Gulf Stream

One of the world's most powerful ocean currents runs through the Bermuda Triangle. The Gulf Stream runs through the Gulf of Mexico and travels northeast past the Florida coast on its way to the northern North Atlantic Ocean. This fast-moving stream of warm water measures up to 50 miles (80 kilometers) wide and has a very powerful pull on all surface vessels. Boats caught in the Gulf Stream can be swept many miles off course. To add to the dangers, towering waves often form on either side of the current.

The strange Sargasso Sea

Close to the center of the Bermuda Triangle is a large area of very calm water covered by floating seaweed. The seaweed is called sargassum, and the area that it covers is called the Sargasso Sea. The Sargasso Sea spreads over an area of roughly 2 million square miles (5.2 million square kilometers) and is surrounded by currents on all sides.

Some people who write about the Bermuda Triangle have described the Sargasso Sea as a place of great horror, where vessels can get caught in huge tangles of weed. In fact, sargassum weed forms small, floating patches that even small boats can pass through easily

▲ The deepest-known blue hole in the world is Dean's Blue Hole, close to Long Island, in the Bahamas. It is 663 feet (202 meters) deep.

Wormholes or caves?

Blue holes look like circular patches of deep-blue water. In the 1990s, some Triangle investigators claimed that these blue holes were entrances to wormholes—secret tunnels leading to another world. However, in the past 30 years, deep-sea divers have begun to investigate blue holes. They have found that the holes are in fact deep underwater caves.

PROFESSOR WHEELER'S WORMHOLES

In 1957, John A. Wheeler, a professor at Princeton University, introduced his theory of wormholes in the universe. He described imaginary wormholes that connect different dimensions of time and space.

Wheeler's wormholes became very popular with science fiction writers, who used them in their stories. The writers described secret tunnels that were used by aliens from outer space to reach people on Earth. However, Professor Wheeler saw his "wormholes" as an abstract idea, meaning they existed only as part of his theory of time and space. He never suggested that they were real tunnels under the sea.

SCIENTIFIC EXPLANATIONS?

Some investigators have tried to find a scientific solution to the Triangle mystery. According to one theory, faulty compass readings are to blame for some of the disasters. Another theory proposes that boats and planes may have been sunk by gases that erupted (burst out) from under the ocean floor. But is there clear evidence to support these theories?

▼ Can some disasters in the Bermuda Triangle be blamed on errors in navigation?

Compass trouble

Up until the end of the 1900s, sailors and pilots relied on compasses to chart their course. They used their compass to show them the direction of "magnetic north." Then they calculated the direction of true north and all the other compass directions.

In most parts of the globe, the distance between magnetic north and true north is quite large. This means that navigators need to make an adjustment to calculate true north. However, in the region close to the Equator, the difference between magnetic and true north is so small that navigators do not need to make their usual adjustment.

▼ Old-fashioned navigators relied on calculating the difference between magnetic north and "true north." This could be confusing in the Triangle area.

Navigation errors?

Is it possible that some navigators in the Bermuda Triangle became confused, and forgot that they should not make their usual compass adjustment? Or would most experienced sailors be aware that they needed to use their compass in a different way in this region?

Using GPS

Today, most sailors and pilots rely on global positioning system (GPS) receivers rather than compasses. GPS receivers pick up information from **satellites** in space and are extremely accurate. So, faulty compass readings are no longer a problem in the Triangle.

▲ Deep-sea divers have discovered pockets of gas trapped under the ocean floor.

Bubbles of gas

Is it possible that exploding bubbles of gas caused some of the disappearances inside the Triangle?

Divers have discovered that there are huge amounts of methane gas (known as methane hydrates) trapped underneath the ocean floor. When the pressure inside these pockets builds up, gas escapes in bubbles and erupts on the surface of the ocean.

Danger from bubbles

Bursting bubbles of gas could put ships and boats in danger. A ship could be sucked beneath the surface. Even planes could be at risk. If the methane gas came into contact with heat from a plane's engines, the plane could easily burst into flames.

Where's the evidence?

There is evidence that vessels have been affected by exploding gas bubbles. Several oil-drilling platforms have collapsed because of releases of gas on the ocean floor. In 2000, divers off the east coast of Scotland found a trawler (a large fishing boat) resting inside a crater filled with methane gas. It is believed that it had been sunk by an enormous bubble of gas.

TESTING THE THEORY

In 2003, scientists at Monash University in Australia conducted an experiment to test the hypothesis that a vessel could be sunk by a bubble of gas. Using a tank and boat made of Perspex (a hard, clear plastic), they observed the effect of bubbles on the boat. By following the scientific method, the scientists came to the conclusion that the boat could be sunk.

▲ In April 2010, there was a huge explosion on board the Deepwater Horizon oil platform. The explosion was probably caused by a bubble of methane gas escaping from under the ocean bed. This blast caused a massive oil spill.

ALIENS AND ATLANTIS?

In the late 1960s and early 1970s, John Wallace Spencer, Charles Berlitz, and Richard Winer all wrote books about the Triangle that included paranormal explanations. One theory claimed that the missing ships and planes could have been abducted (stolen away) by aliens from other planets. This theory was very popular with science fiction fans, but can it stand up to the test of science?

▼ Were ships in the Triangle really beamed up to space by aliens?

Stolen by aliens?

People who believe in UFOs say that these spacecraft could have the power to beam up ships and planes. But they do not present any evidence for their theory.

It has also been suggested that aliens might use wormholes to draw their victims into another world. You can read about wormholes on page 27.

UFOs in the Triangle?

Is it possible that aliens visit the Triangle in their spacecraft? There have been many reports of unidentified flying objects (UFOs) in the region. One of the best-known sightings took place in 1971, when members of the crew of the USS *John F. Kennedy* reported seeing a glowing disc hovering over the sea. However, their ship did not experience any problems in the Triangle.

When investigations are carried out into sightings of UFOs, investigators usually discover that people have been confused. They may have seen an unusual cloud formation. Or they may have spotted a meteor, which is a piece of rock that falls from space and burns up as it enters Earth's atmosphere. Yet, despite this evidence, some people remain convinced that alien spacecraft really exist.

▲ Some writers have claimed that aliens kidnapped the members of Flight 19 (see pages 6 to 9). The movie director Steven Spielberg used this theory as the basis of his science fiction movie *Close Encounters of the Third Kind*.

The power of Atlantis?

Some people claim that the legendary kingdom of Atlantis holds the key to the mystery of the Bermuda Triangle. According to ancient legend, Atlantis was buried under the ocean thousands of years ago. It has been suggested that the kingdom of Atlantis could lie directly beneath the Bermuda Triangle.

Some people claim that the people of Atlantis have never died. They believe that these ancient people are still living under the ocean today. They also suggest that the people of Atlantis could be using their mysterious powers inside the Bermuda Triangle.

Evidence from Atlantis?

An American man named Edgar Cayce claimed he could talk directly to the people of Atlantis, and between the years 1924 and 1944 he revealed many "messages" from them. Cayce claimed that the people of Atlantis were beaming rays of energy from a mysterious crystal. He also predicted that researchers would discover the western edge of Atlantis near the coast of Bimini Island, in the heart of the Bermuda Triangle.

Proof from Atlantis?

In 1968, divers found ruins on the ocean floor close to Bimini. The ruins seemed to be part of an enormous city wall. Some people believed that the ruins were proof that Atlantis had once existed under the Bermuda Triangle. However, most geologists (scientists who study rock) think that the wall of rock was formed by nature.

In 1975, a diver named Dr. Ray Brown claimed that he found a temple shaped like a pyramid in the ocean near Bimini. Inside the temple was a crystal ball, which Brown brought back to the surface. He kept the crystal a secret for several years before displaying it to "believers." The believers claimed it had very unusual powers.

▲ Is there evidence beneath the Atlantic Ocean that Atlantis really did exist?

HUMAN CAUSES?

Is it possible to blame human behavior for most of the disasters in the Triangle? Bad decisions or carelessness have certainly played a part in many accidents inside the Triangle. Other possible causes of "disappearances" are piracy and warfare. This chapter will consider all these explanations.

A bad decision

Even very experienced navigators sometimes make mistakes—especially in difficult weather. On January 1, 1958, businessman Harvey Conover sailed his yacht, the *Revonoc*, directly into a storm. Unsurprisingly, Conover and his yacht were never seen again. Some journalists blamed the disappearance on mysterious forces, but others came to the conclusion that simple human error was to blame. It appeared that Conover had made the wrong decision to brave the storm and trust in his own skills.

▲ Some of the disasters that happened in the Triangle must have been the result of simple human error.

▲ These coast guardsmen examine two life preservers and a foghorn from the sunken *Marine Sulphur Queen*. Some writers claimed the sinking of this tanker in 1963 was a mystery "disappearance." In fact, the tanker was unfit to go to sea. One crew member called it "a floating garbage can."

A careless crew

In 1972, the tanker *V. A. Fogg* suddenly exploded off the Florida coast. Some reporters claimed that the mysterious Triangle had claimed more victims. But these claims were disproved when local coast guards conducted a thorough investigation. The investigation revealed that the crew had failed to follow the proper method for cleaning out benzene, a very dangerous gas, from the ship's tanks.

MISTAKES ON FLIGHT 19

Human error was probably to blame for the fate of Flight 19 (see pages 6 to 9). An investigation revealed that the flight instructor, Charles Taylor, was not familiar with the Triangle region, and he had a history of sometimes being a careless navigator.

Pirates

Some disappearances inside the Triangle may have been the work of pirates. Until the 1900s, piracy was common in the Caribbean and the surrounding areas. Any ship with a valuable load was at risk from pirates, who would board the ship, kill the crew, and take everything they could. Sometimes pirates took over a ship. Sometimes they simply left it to drift.

PIRATES ON THE GHOST SHIP?

People have suggested that the "ghost ship" found by the crew of the *Ellen Austin* had been attacked by pirates, who stole the ship's cargo and killed the crew. (See pages 10 to 13 for this story.) However, the crew of the *Ellen Austin* reported that the ghost ship was not damaged in any way. There was no evidence that it had been attacked by pirates.

Smugglers

Since the 1970s, drug smugglers have been active in the Caribbean and Bermuda Triangle regions. These smugglers sometimes steal pleasure boats to transport illegal drugs from Central America to the United States. Smugglers may have been involved in some disappearances of yachts and crews inside the Triangle.

Fighting at sea

Many losses inside the Triangle have happened in times of war. Records from World War I (1914–1918) and World War II (1939–1945) give war-related explanations for the loss of dozens of ships and planes inside the Bermuda Triangle. However, the fate of three U.S. ships has never been completely explained.

The U.S. ship *Cyclops* disappeared in 1918, during World War I, and the *Proteus* and *Nereus* both vanished in 1941, during World War II. Some writers have claimed that the disappearance of these three ships is a mystery. But it is possible that they were attacked and sunk by German submarines.

▼ Could German submarines have sunk three U.S. ships, which appeared to have vanished without a trace?

IS THERE REALLY A MYSTERY?

Some investigators have asked the question: Is there really a mystery to be solved? Then they have made a careful examination of the evidence.

Checking the facts

People who believe in the mystery of the Triangle list a large number of "disappearances." But is there hard evidence for these events? Investigators, such as pilot and librarian Larry Kusche, have double-checked the newspaper reports of the time. They have discovered that many of the ships recorded as "missing without a trace" were in fact later reported to be found again.

Comparing records

Investigators have also compared the list of "disappearances" with the records for shipping in the region. They have checked the reports of local coast guards, who note all shipwrecks and accidents at sea. Some investigators have also examined the records of ship insurers, who pay out money to owners of ships that are damaged or lost. These investigations reveal that many reports of "disappearances" cannot be proven.

Myth-buster

Accident black spot?

The Triangle area is one of the busiest transportation zones in the world, providing the main route between North America and the Caribbean. Considering the amount of traffic in the area, the number of accidents is surprisingly low.

Looking at the bigger picture

It is often claimed that the Bermuda Triangle has an unusually high number of accidents. But is this claim really true? Investigators have calculated the amount of traffic passing through the region and compared this figure with the number of reported accidents. They have reached the conclusion that the accident rate in the Triangle is no higher than in any other region of the world.

CAN THE MYSTERY BE SOLVED?

This book has examined a range of responses to the mystery of the Bermuda Triangle. But which ideas make the most sense to you?

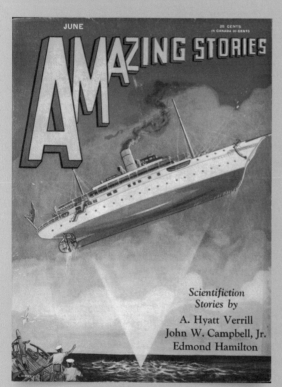

▲ Some theories about the Bermuda Triangle are very exciting. But do they stand up to the tests of science and common sense?

JUNE — 25 CENTS IN CANADA 30 CENTS

AMAZING STORIES

Scientifiction Stories by
A. Hyatt Verrill
John W. Campbell, Jr.
Edmond Hamilton

All sorts of solutions

Do you think the disappearances can be explained by the weird weather in the region? Do you think the ocean is partly to blame, with its treacherous currents and hungry sharks? Can some accidents be blamed on problems with compass readings? And is it possible that bubbles of methane gas could cause some disasters?

Some people prefer a more imaginative approach to the mystery. Does the answer lie in wormholes leading to another dimension of time and space? Or could the disappearances be due to aliens or "death-rays" from Atlantis?

Finally, there is the suggestion that human beings have caused most of the disasters in the Triangle. Are bad decisions and carelessness to blame? And were some disappearances acts of piracy or war?

There is also the suggestion that the mystery does not in fact exist. The evidence presented on pages 40 to 41 suggests that many apparent facts about "disappearances" and other events cannot be proved.

A scientific approach

The best way to approach all these theories is to apply the scientific method. Ask yourself: Can the theory be tested? What evidence is used to construct the hypothesis, and can it be trusted? Once you have asked these questions, you can reach a conclusion.

You may decide that several of the theories provide good explanations for the strange events in the Triangle. Or you may reach the conclusion that there is no mystery to be solved. In the end, you must make up your own mind about the question of the Bermuda Triangle.

TIMELINE

1881
The crew of the *Ellen Austin* meet a ghost ship in the Bermuda Triangle.

1918
The U.S. ship *Cyclops* disappears in the Triangle area.

1924
Edgar Cayce starts to reveal his "messages" from Atlantis.

1941
The U.S. ships *Proteus* and *Nereus* disappear.

1945
U.S. Navy training Flight 19 disappears.

During the search for Flight 19, a seaplane explodes.

1948
The airliner *Star Tiger* disappears.

1949
A DC3 passenger plane disappears.

1952
Journalist George X. Sand introduces the idea of the Bermuda Triangle.

1955
The pleasure yacht *Connemara IV* is found adrift with no crew.

1958
Harvey Conover and his yacht, the *Revonoc*, disappear.

1963
The U.S. tanker *Marine Sulphur Queen* disappears.

1964
Vincent Gaddis writes an article called "The Deadly Bermuda Triangle," listing many mysterious incidents.

1969
John Wallace Spencer publishes *Limbo of the Lost*, introducing the theory of alien abductions (kidnappings).

1970
Pilot Bruce Gernon flies into an "electronic fog" but survives.

1972
The tanker *V. A. Fogg* explodes off the Florida coast.

1974
Charles Berlitz publishes *The Bermuda Triangle*, and Richard Winer publishes *The Devil's Triangle*. Both books explore paranormal explanations for the Triangle mystery.

1975
Larry Kusche writes *The Bermuda Triangle Mystery: Solved*, in which he disproves most of the Triangle theories.

1993
A company called Equinox produces a TV documentary providing explanations for the Bermuda Triangle.

SUMMING UP
THE SCIENCE

Stormy weather is the cause of many accidents in the Bermuda Triangle. But why are storms in this region so severe?

Tropical weather

The Bermuda Triangle lies in the region called the tropics. This is an area on either side of the equator (an imaginary line around Earth), between the Tropic of Cancer and the Tropic of Capricorn. Within the tropics, the weather is very hot, and powerful winds blow across the ocean. There are frequent storms at sea, caused by differences in air temperature as cool winds meet warm water. These usually take a circular form and are known as **tropical cyclones**.

How do tropical cyclones form?

Cyclones form when layers of cool air blow across warm water. Warm air rising up from the ocean is caught up in the winds and whirled around rapidly. The droplets in the air cool to form cloud, and the clouds grow heavy and produce rain. The cyclone hovers just above the waves and is blown across the ocean by surface winds.

GLOSSARY

blue hole entrance to an underwater cave, which looks from the surface like a circular patch of deep-blue water

compass instrument (tool) used for finding directions with a magnetic needle that always points north

conclusion decision that is made after gathering and testing evidence

crew team of people who all work together, especially on a ship or plane

current powerful flow of water in an ocean or a river

cyclone very strong wind blowing in a spiral (cone shape)

dimension space in which things happen

disprove prove or show that something is not true

electronic relating to electricity. Electronic machines work by using small amounts of electricity.

erupt burst out with great force

evidence information and facts that help to prove something

experiment scientific test to try out a theory

ghost ship ship with nobody on board that seems to have a crew of ghosts

hypothesis idea that a scientist suggests and then tries to prove

magnetic north place on the globe that all magnets point to. The position of magnetic north is gradually moving, but it is over 1,000 miles (1,600 kilometers) away from the North Pole.

methane type of gas made by living things when they rot and decay

navigator someone who steers a ship or a plane, using instruments (tools) such as a compass

paranormal not normal and not easily explained by the laws of nature

piracy act of being a pirate and attacking ships at sea in order to steal their goods

predict say what will happen in the future

satellite machine that is sent into orbit around Earth

schooner old-fashioned sailing ship, with many masts and sails

science fiction stories about life in the future or life on other planets

scientific method way of testing a theory, using evidence and experiments, before reaching a conclusion

tanker ship with large tanks that is used to carry liquids or gases

theory idea that aims to explain something

time warp kink or bend in time that makes time behave very strangely

treacherous looking safe, but actually being very dangerous

tropical relating to the hot, rainy area on either side of the equator, between the Tropic of Cancer and the Tropic of Capricorn

vessel any kind of ship or boat

wormhole tunnel that may lead into surprising places

yacht large sailing boat